Hop, Swim and Run

Margaret Clyne

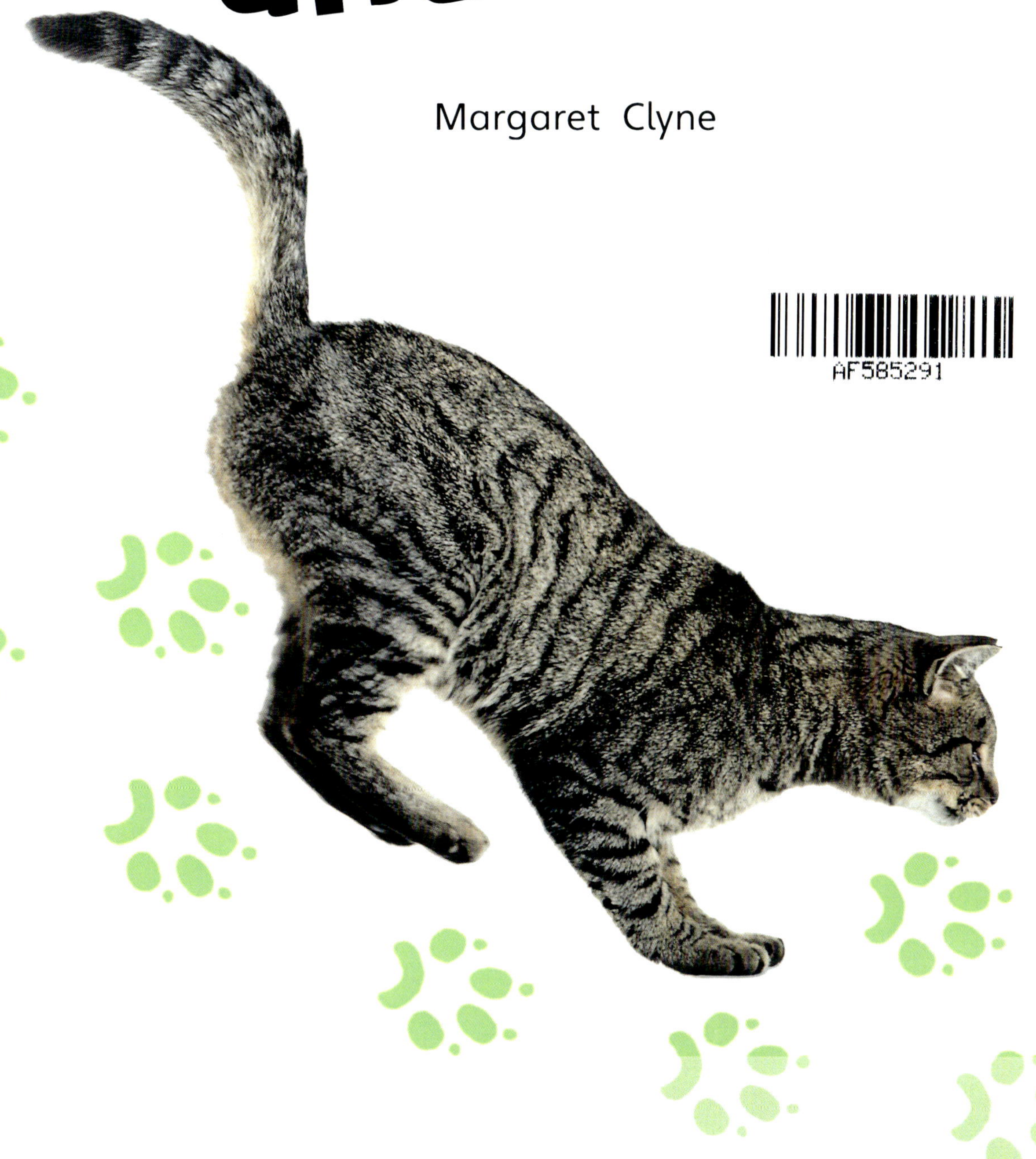

AF585291

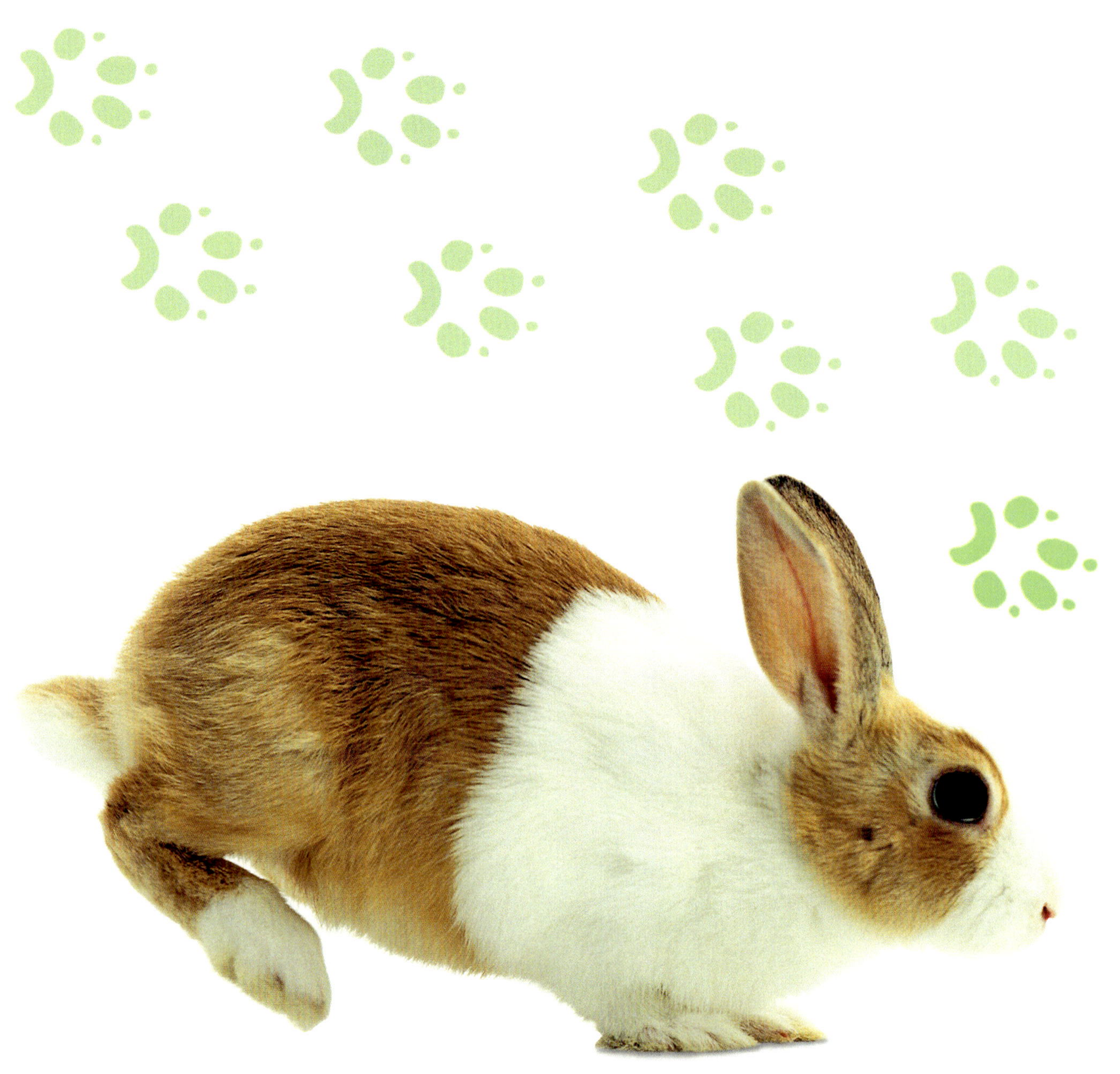

This is a rabbit.
It can hop.

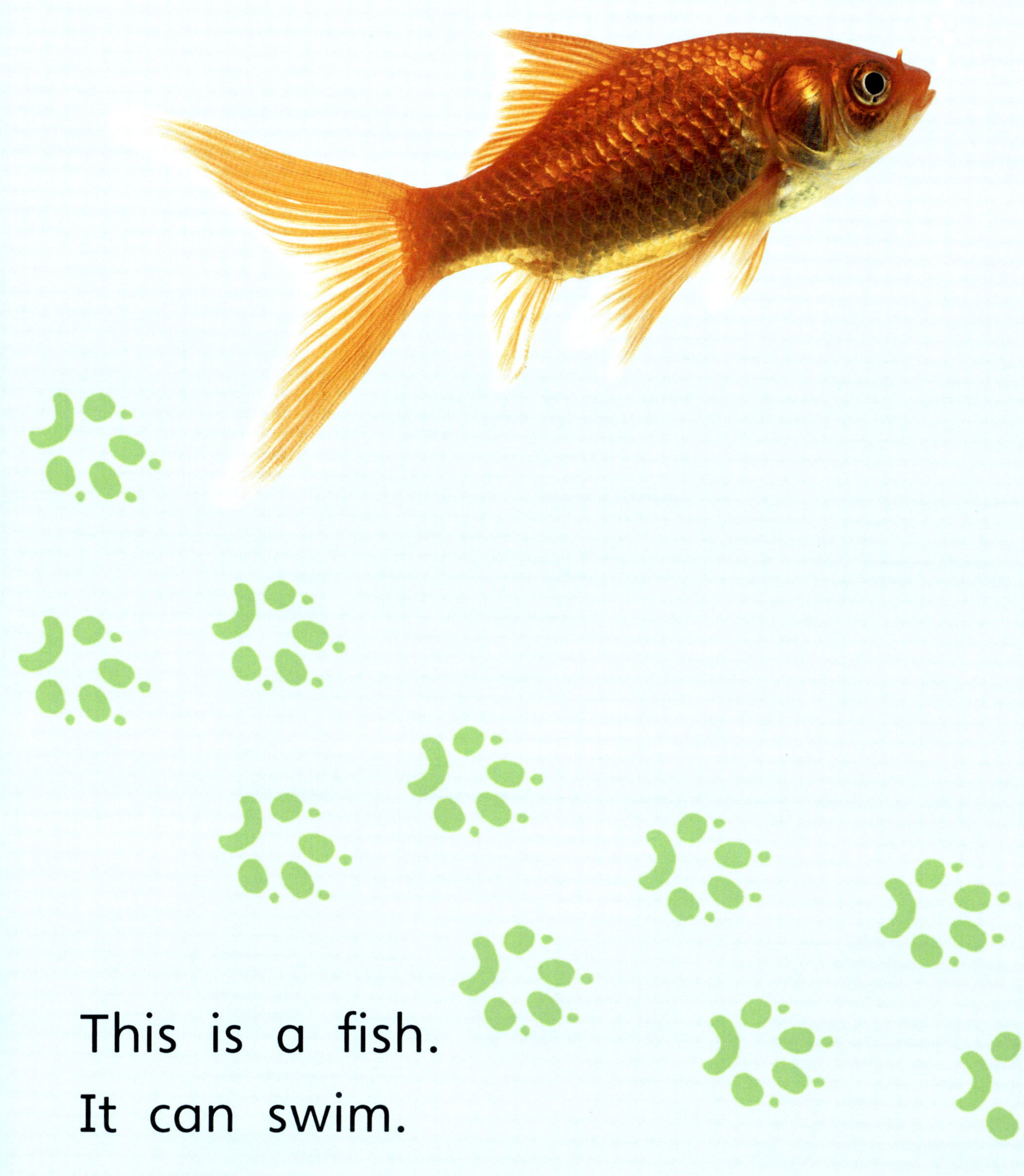

This is a fish.
It can swim.

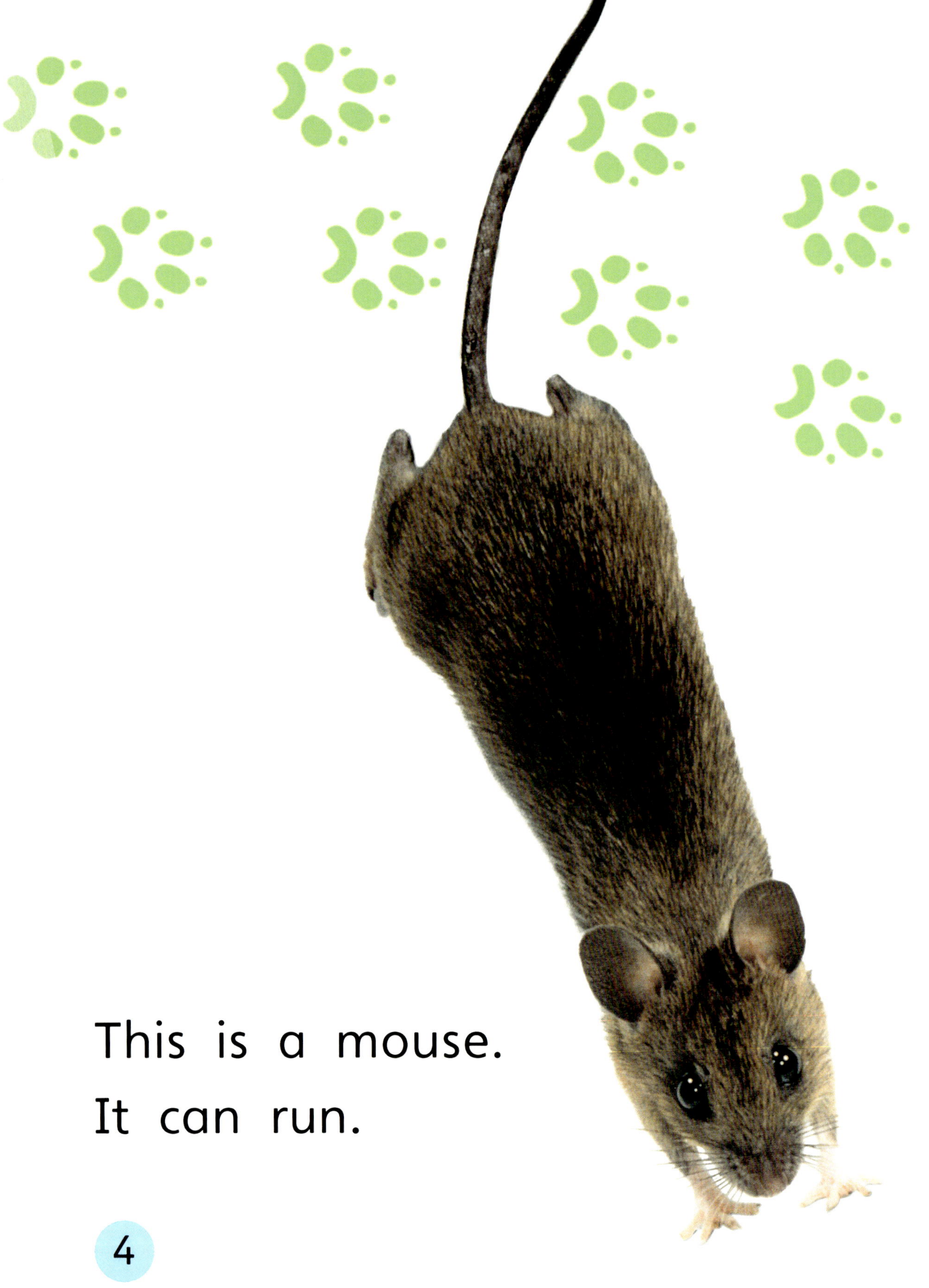

This is a mouse.
It can run.

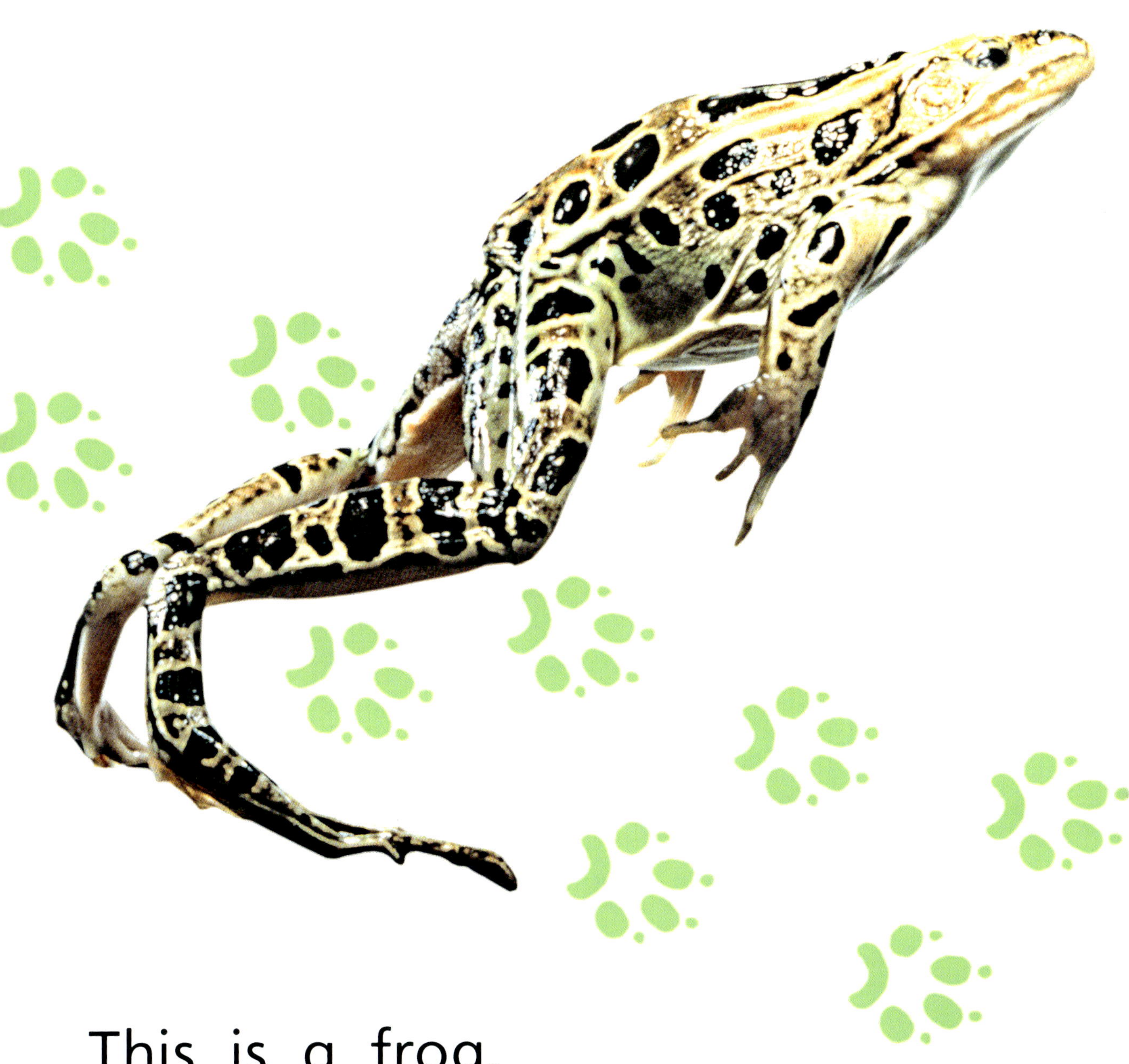

This is a frog.
It can hop.

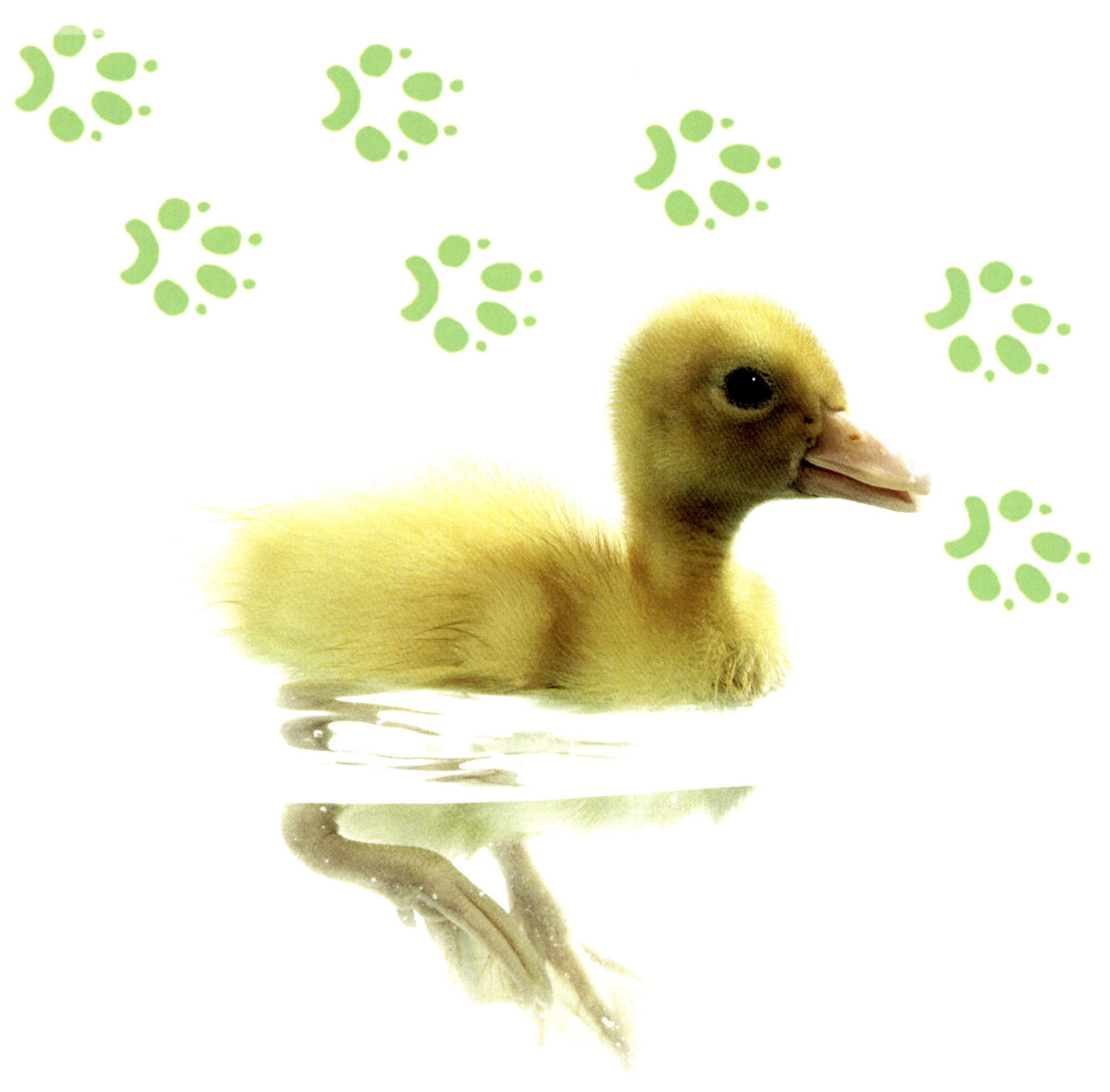

This is a duck.
It can swim.

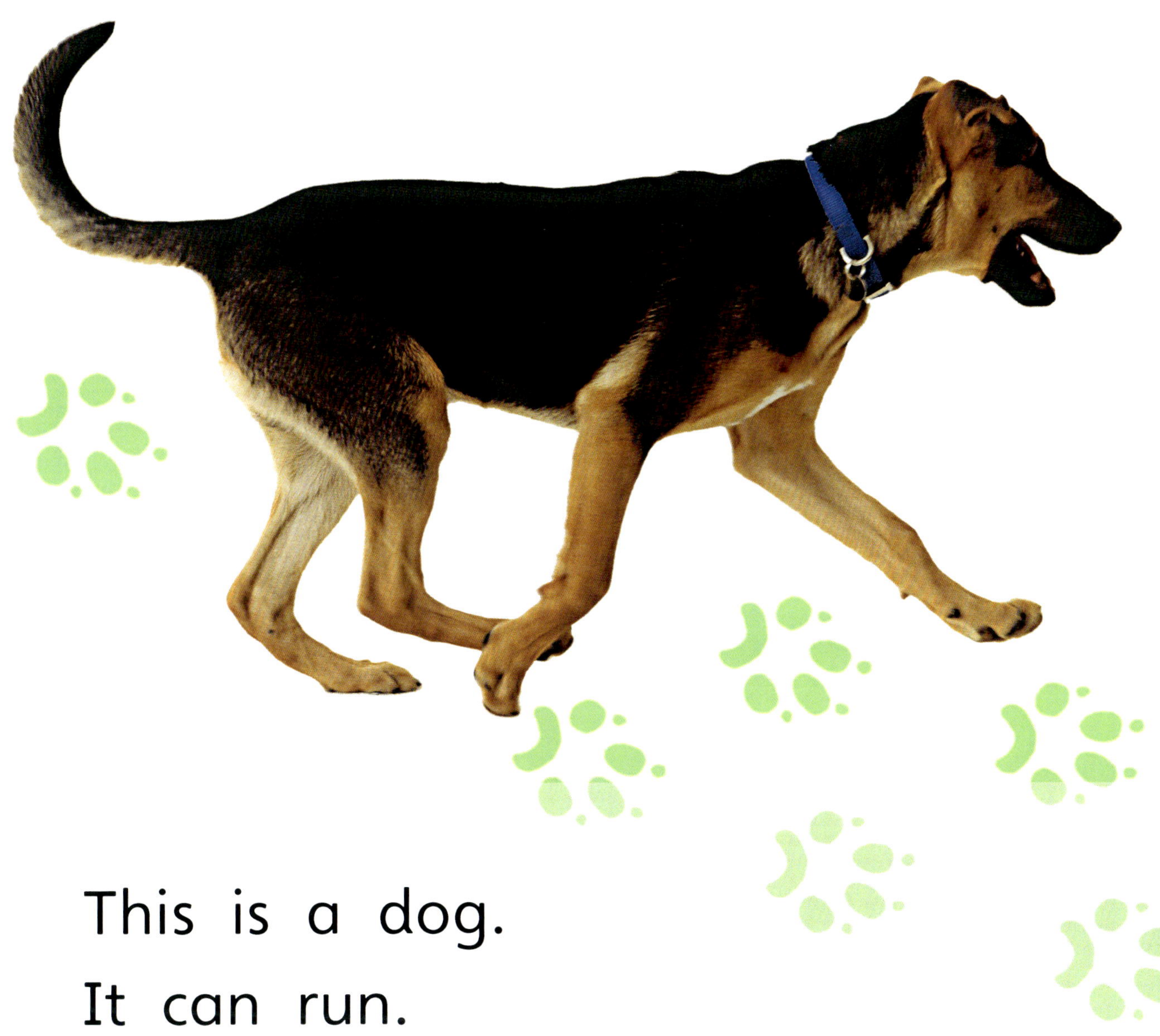

This is a dog.
It can run.

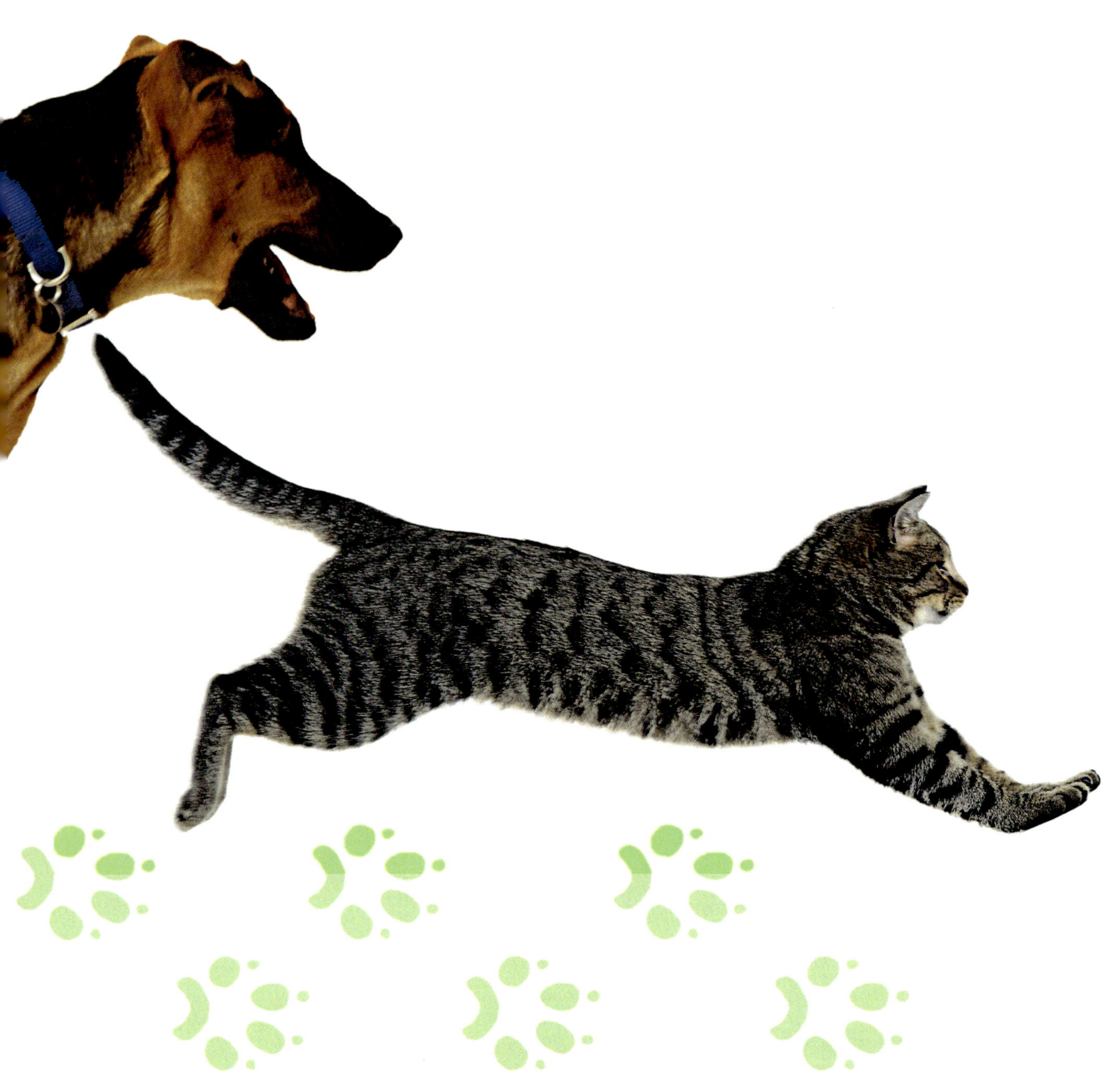

This cat can run, too.